GREAT DISASTERS

THE ERUPTION OF
KRAKATOA

RUPERT MATTHEWS

Illustrated by

TONY SMITH and PETER BULL

The Bookwright Press
New York · 1989

Great Disasters

The Chernobyl Catastrophe
The Hindenburg Tragedy
The Eruption of Krakatoa
The Fire of London

The Destruction of Pompeii
The San Francisco Earthquake
The Space Shuttle Disaster
The Sinking of the Titanic

First published in the
United States in 1989 by
The Bookwright Press
387 Park Avenue South
New York, NY 10016

First published in 1988 by
Wayland (Publishers) Limited
61 Western Road, Hove
East Sussex BN3 1JD

Front cover *The eruption caused a giant rolling wave, or* **tsunami**, *that destroyed thousands of boats and hundreds of coastal villages and towns.*

Words that are printed in **bold** the first time they appear in the text are explained in the glossary.

Library of Congress Cataloging-in-Publication Data

Matthews, Rupert.
   The eruption of Krakatoa/Rupert Matthews: illustrated by Tony Smith.
     p.   cm. — (Great disasters)
   Bibliography: p.
   Includes index.
   ISBN 0-531-18239-8
   1. Krakatoa (Indonesia) — Eruption, 1883 — Juvenile literature.
I. Smith, Tony II. Title. III. Series.
QE523.K73M38 1989
959.8—dc 19   88-4100
                                       CIP
                                       AC

Phototypeset by Oliver Dawkins Ltd, Burgess Hill,
West Sussex
Printed in Italy by G. Canale & C.S.p.A, Turin

CONTENTS

A SURVIVOR'S STORY

This is how one of the very few survivors of the eruption at Krakatoa might have told her story.

"The worst day of my life began so quietly. At midday, there was no indication of what was going to happen. Nobody thought that the mountain was dangerous.

"From our house, we could see the top of Krakatoa **volcano** quite easily. It rose up above the forests and was a clear landmark.

When my father went out fishing he was always able to keep the summit of Krakatoa in sight, even when he went to the fishing grounds farthest away from the island.

"On Sunday afternoon, smoke started to pour out of the volcano. Some people were worried, but most ignored the smoke. It did not seem very dangerous. But as daylight of the next morning began to arrive, the earth shook several times. Father said that we ought to leave and go to stay with his brother in Java. Mother and I quickly gathered up our belongings.

"We ran down to the beach and got into father's boat. As we set sail, the ground shook again. Mother looked very frightened as we moved out to sea. There were many other boats sailing away from the island.

"We had been sailing for about two hours when it happened. The island of Krakatoa was on the horizon. Suddenly, the whole mountain burst apart. A huge column of smoke and fire leapt upward. Where the island had been only moments earlier, there was now a huge burning ball of fire and smoke.

Many fled from Krakatoa in their fishing boats when the eruption began.

"I called to my father, who turned to look at Krakatoa. Then the noise of the explosion hit us. It was so loud that I had to hold my hands over my ears. After the explosion I couldn't hear anything. Even now I cannot hear properly. The people in the other boats were staring at the island.

"My father sat down in the boat and hugged my mother. I continued to stare at the smoke and fire of Krakatoa. As I watched, the ocean in front of me seemed to change. It was rising upward. A huge wave, as big as a mountain, was rushing toward us. I felt our boat being lifted high upward as the wave struck. When our boat reached the crest of the wave, I looked down behind us and felt dizzy.

"I am not sure what happened next. Our boat was flipped over and I felt myself being dragged underwater. I desperately held my breath. Then suddenly I reached the surface and could breathe again.

"I looked around me. The boat had gone. All the boats had disappeared; the terrific wave must have smashed them all to pieces. A large piece of wood was floating near me and I grabbed hold of it. I looked around and saw my father swimming toward me. We kept afloat by holding onto the wood. We could see a few other people nearby, but there was no sign of mother. After several hours, a large ship came by and picked us up. Father and I were safe at last, and when we found mother on the same boat, we were so happy. Even though we had lost our home, at least we would be together."

Passing ships picked up survivors of the disaster from the open sea.

LIFE ON KRAKATOA

By 1883, Krakatoa was supporting a thriving and prosperous population. Many villages were scattered along the shores or among the fields. Hundreds of people lived on the island of Krakatoa. Their lives were peaceful and pleasant.

Krakatoa lay between the **Indonesian** islands of Java and Sumatra. It had very **fertile** soil in which crops grew easily. The climate also helped the farmers of Krakatoa. Temperatures were warm all year and heavy rains fell on the island during the **monsoon** season. These conditions were perfect for the cultivation of rice. Large fields, or **paddies**, of rice, were spread across the lower areas of Krakatoa.

Below *Indonesia;* **inset** *the location of Krakatoa in the Sunda Straits between the islands of Java and Sumatra.*

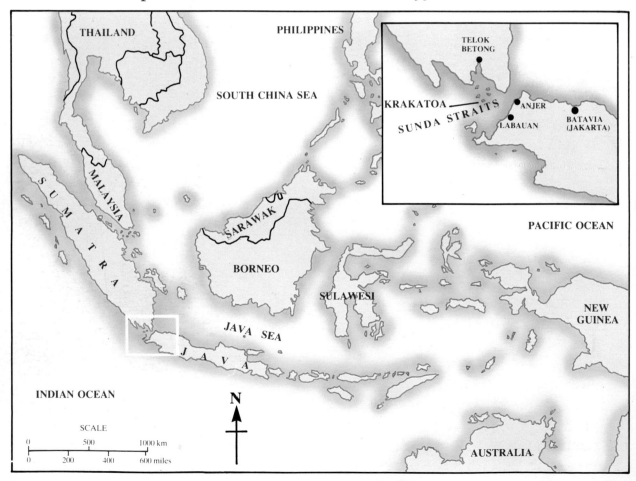

8

Farming and fishing

Although they used hand tools and techniques that would appear old-fashioned today, the farmers of Krakatoa produced far more rice than they and their families needed. Much of this was **exported** to neighboring islands in exchange for the goods that they lacked on Krakatoa.

There were abundant fishing grounds in the waters around the island. From many coastal villages, fishermen put out to sea in canoes. These wooden craft were powered by large triangular sails and their hulls were made from hollowed-out tree trunks. Small wooden **outriggers** projected on either side, making the craft far more stable than single-bodied canoes.

This enabled the fishermen to cast their nets without worrying about overturning their craft. The canoes were superbly adapted for fishing around Krakatoa.

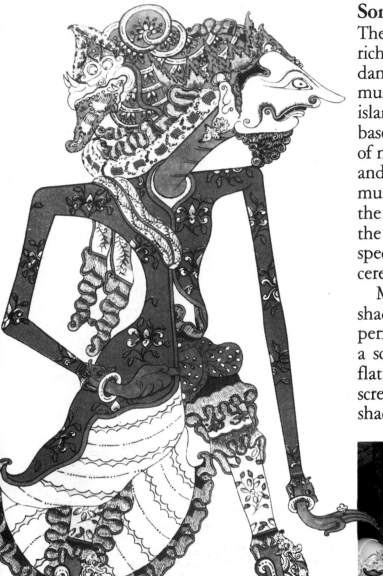

Song and dance

The people of Krakatoa had developed a rich artistic culture that centered around dancing and music. The most distinctive music of Krakatoa and neighboring islands was gamelan. This style of music is based upon percussion instruments made of metal, which resemble cymbals, gongs and **xylophones**. Often, singers joined the musicians for performances. Together with the intricate **ritual dancing** of Indonesia, the gamelan was usually performed on special occasions, such as religious ceremonies.

More common in everyday life were the shadow puppet shows. These were performed by showmen equipped with a screen and a bright lamp. By placing flat puppets between the lamp and the screen, the skillful puppeteer uses the shadows of the puppets to act out plays.

Above *A Javanese shadow puppet. The white areas are transparent, allowing light to shine through.* **Right** *Java also has puppets more familiar to the West.*

Above *A circle of dancers in traditional costume performing a spectacular Indonesian ritual dance.*

Right *Assorted gongs, cymbals and drums are the standard instruments in a gamelan orchestra.*

Performed at night, these shows were popular on Krakatoa.

In 1883, whether they were farmers or fishermen, the people of Krakatoa led prosperous and enjoyable lives. They can have had no idea of the disaster that was about to overwhelm them.

EARLY RUMBLINGS

Krakatoa's history

The island that existed in 1883 was the result of more than a million years of volcanic activity. Originally there had been no island at all, simply an area of sea between the islands of Java and Sumatra. But about a million years ago a crack opened in the **earth's crust**, and **lava** and other volcanic material were forced through this opening.

Over hundreds of thousands of years, this material continued to pour out of the earth and to solidify on the ocean bed. Eventually, so much matter collected that it formed a large island. This island was then eroded away until only a partially submerged volcanic **crater** remained. Forsaken Island and Lang Island were, in 1883, the remnants of this **caldera**.

Fresh volcanic activity then began and it continued for several thousand more years.

Below *Krakatoa lies on a junction of two geological plates.*

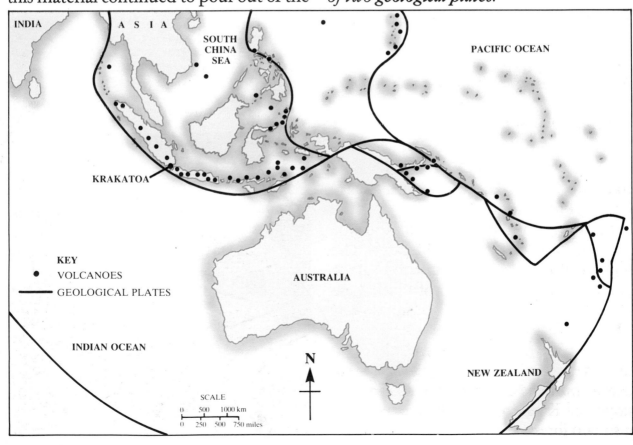

KEY
• VOLCANOES
— GEOLOGICAL PLATES

INDIA

ASIA

SOUTH CHINA SEA

PACIFIC OCEAN

KRAKATOA

AUSTRALIA

INDIAN OCEAN

N

NEW ZEALAND

SCALE
0   500   1000 km
0   250   500   750 miles

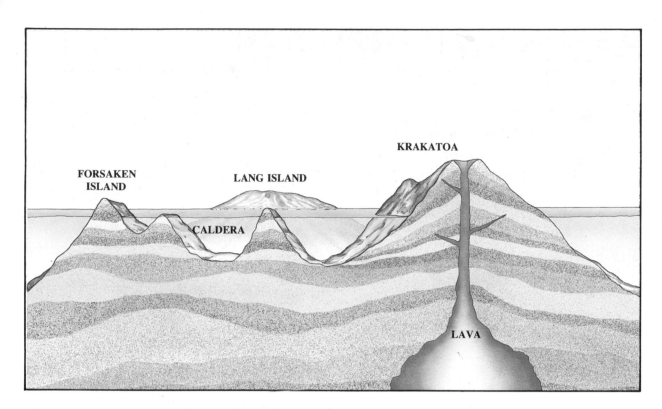

Labels in figure: FORSAKEN ISLAND, LANG ISLAND, KRAKATOA, CALDERA, LAVA

Above *A cross section through Krakatoa.*

Right *Javan rain forest.*

A large new island was built up inside the crater of the ancient volcano. This island became known as Krakatoa.

Running along the center of Krakatoa was a line of volcanic peaks and craters. The highest of these summits towered 820 m (2,700 ft). The volcanic rock of which these mountains were formed weathered readily into soil. Rich in the chemicals that help plants to grow, the soil that formed proved to be very fertile. For thousands of years, before humans came to the island, the slopes of Krakatoa were blanketed with lush rain forest.

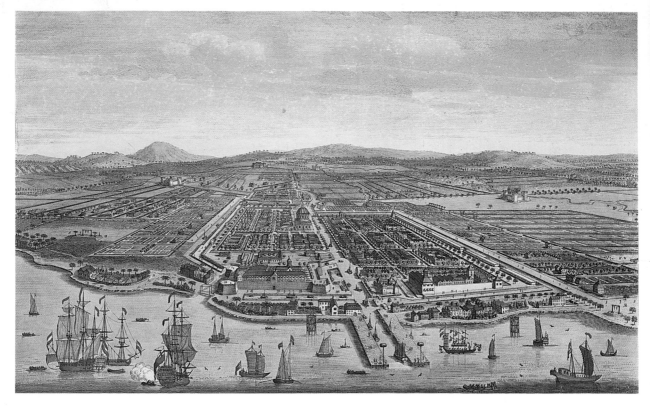

Above *The port of Batavia, capital of Indonesia in 1780.*

Below *Krakatoan fishing villages would have looked like this.*

People discover the island

When groups of farmers first arrived on the island, perhaps 5,000 years ago, they felled large areas of forest. On this cleared land they grew rice and other crops. Like the forest before, the crops grew fast on the fertile volcanic soil.

However, the volcanoes of Krakatoa were still active while the early farmers lived on the island. Even until 1680 occasional eruptions poured out hot ash and lava onto the island.

In the years that followed, some islanders may have forgotten that their island was, in fact, a volcano. This was because for more than 200 years Krakatoa was **dormant**.

Right *A typical Javan village at the time of the eruption.*

Below *Three stages in the formation of Krakatoa.*
1) The island formed by eruptions.
2) The island before the arrival of humans. Dense rain forest covers the island.
3) The island on the eve of the eruption. Over the centuries, most of the forest has been cleared by the islanders to make way for villages and fields.

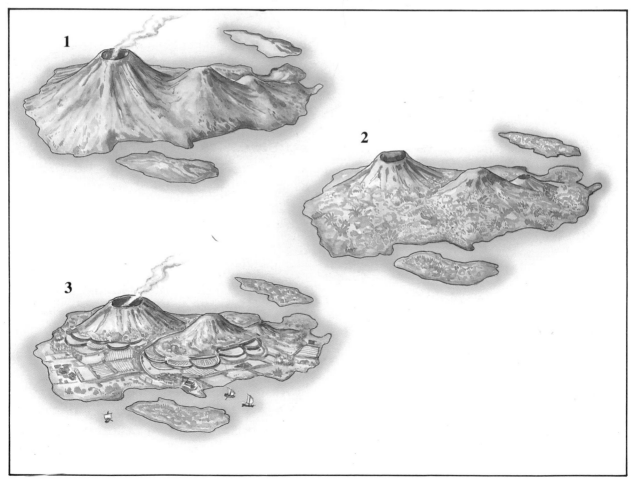

Above *Smoke pours from the active volcano Mount Bromo, on Java, in 1988.*
Below *A drawing from a photograph of the eruption of May 20, 1883.*

The volcano comes alive

Krakatoa came violently to life on May 20, 1883. A loud roar crashed through the air. A massive column of ash and smoke shot upward from the center of the island. The islanders must have been taken by surprise, as few would have known anything about volcanoes. However, the volcanic activity soon faded away. Over the following weeks several other minor eruptions occurred, but these were only a taste of what was to come.

On the afternoon of August 26, 1883, a violent explosion shook the island. A vast cloud of ash and smoke shot into the sky.

Further explosions rang out as night fell over Krakatoa. A visiting Englishman wrote that the people who were on the island " . . . made the scene dismal with their cries and prayers." Many climbed into boats and fled the island.

Even out at sea, the events of the night of August 26 were dramatic. Seamen on a ship about 16 km (10 mi) from shore were watching the eruption when they noticed that the sea was warm. Clearly, something very unusual and powerful was happening at Krakatoa.

Below *Krakatoans praying for help on the night of August 26, 1883, just a few hours before the explosion.*

Above *A modern photograph shows how red-hot lava cuts through dense jungle, setting fire to the trees.*

THE BLAST

Throughout the night of August 26 and the early morning of the following day, explosions continued to shake Krakatoa. The large plume of smoke and ash rose high into the sky. The people who lived on Krakatoa fled the island or tried to seek shelter as best as they could.

At 10 o'clock in the morning of August 27 all the volcanic activity at Krakatoa that had occurred in the previous hours paled into insignificance as the island blew itself apart.

The blast that ripped through Krakatoa island has never since been equaled.

The destructive power unleashed by the explosion is estimated to have been thousands of times as powerful as the **atomic bombs** dropped on Japan by the United States in 1945 during the World War II. In an instant, most of Krakatoa simply ceased to exist. A large part of the island sank beneath the sea.

The eruption destroyed the island and killed everybody left on shore. Two-thirds of the island were pulverized and thrown 80 km (50 mi) into the air. This immense cloud of dust and rock particles blotted out the sun and spread quickly downwind. More than 240 km (150 mi) away, darkness fell as if night had fallen.

A devastating blast tore Krakatoa apart. Lang island and Forsaken Island **(bottom left and right)** *were later hit by the* **tsunami**.

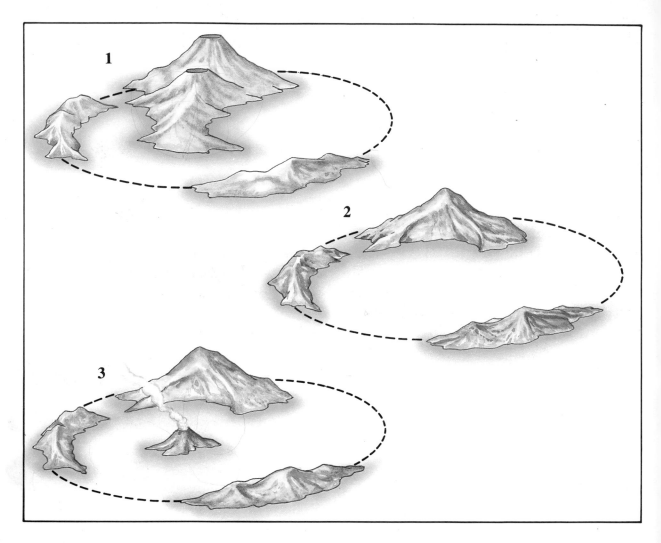

The noise of the blast was tremendous. In Batavia (the capital of Java), 150 km (90 mi) from Krakatoa, people in the street had to cover their ears, but they would have had no idea what they were hearing.

At the town of Macassar (on Sulawesi Island), nearly 1,600 km (1,000 mi) distant, the noise was thought to be coming from a nearby explosion. Ships put out to sea to try to find the cause of the noise. Four hours after the blast occurred,

Above *1) before the eruption,*
2) immediately afterward and
3) today (see page 28).

it was heard on the island of Rodrigues. This island lies 4,776 km (3,000 mi) from Krakatoa. The people of Rodrigues thought they were hearing gunfire from a naval battle beyond the horizon. No doubt they wondered who had started a war without their knowledge.

The wave

At Krakatoa a huge hole had been ripped in the earth's crust. Where an island 820 m (2,700 ft) high had stood, there appeared a crater 6.5 km (4 mi) across and 300 m (980 ft) deep. Seawater was thrown outward by the blast, then fell back into the crater. These movements set up a huge wave, or **tsunami**, which swept out from Krakatoa.

More than 30 m (100 ft) tall, the wave rushed ashore onto the coasts of Java, Sumatra and other nearby islands. This powerful mass of water smashed everything in its path. Whole villages were destroyed and their populations drowned. Large ships were carried far inland — one was found over a mile from the seashore.

Above *A British newspaper reports the eruption. The picture shows Krakatoa shortly before August 27, 1883.*

Below *A map showing the areas affected by the ash and noise.*

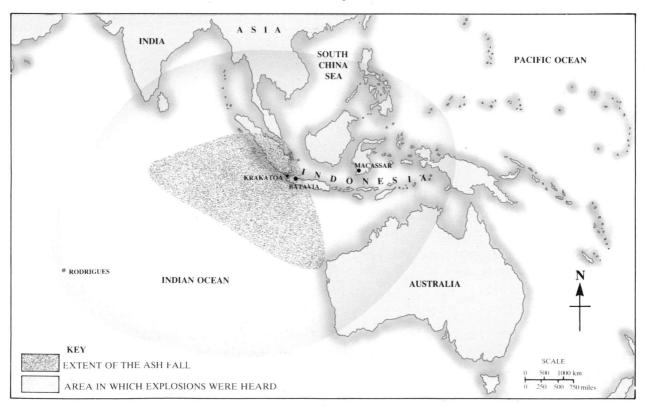

21

A Dutchman named de Vries was in the Javan town of Anjer when the wave struck. De Vries managed to scramble to high ground and climb a tree before the tsunami arrived. He later wrote that he saw " . . . an immense, enormous mass of water, appearing at first mountain high, rush on with a fearful roar and lightning-like rapidity . . . The large roof of a house on bamboo posts came floating toward where my tree stood . . . I looked around. A frightful sight met my eyes. Where Anjer had stood I saw nothing but a foaming and rushing flood."

Terrible scenes such as this were repeated along coasts throughout the region. Hundreds of villages were destroyed and 36,000 people were killed by the tsunami. The wave was so powerful that it was noticed in Panama and the Hawaiian Islands. Even in Britain, scientists detected it. The explosion at Krakatoa was among the most destructive ever recorded.

The narrow escape of de Vries at Anjer.

THE AFTERMATH

The explosion of Krakatoa and the massive wave it created, devastated the surrounding area. A few days after the blast, a Dutchman named van Sandick sailed around the islands. He wrote: "The coasts of Java, as those of Sumatra, were entirely destroyed. The villages and trees had disappeared, we could not even see any ruins, for the waves had demolished and swallowed up the inhabitants, the homes and plantations. This was truly a scene from the **Last Judgement**."

The survivors

The few people who had managed to escape to high ground before the wave struck were reluctant to return to their homes. Most of their friends and families had been killed, and they feared that further eruptions might lead to another terrible wave. For many years the coasts of the islands remained scarcely populated.

With their homes and means of earning a living destroyed, the survivors became **refugees**. The **Dutch colonial government** stepped in to help. Food was distributed to those left homeless, and aid was given to help them to rebuild their lives.

Right *Relief workers measure out rice to be handed out to refugees.*
Below *Colonial government buildings in Batavia, center for the relief operation.*

The dust cloud

Less destructive than the tsunami, but more far reaching, were the effects of the dust cloud thrown up by the blast. The debris had been forced so high into the air, that it became caught in the air streams of the upper atmosphere. In this way the dust was blown around the world.

The most noticeable feature of the dust in the upper atmosphere was the way that it affected sunsets. All over the world, the evening sun glowed brighter than usual. Vivid hues of red, purple and pink were seen at sunset. Evening became a truly spectacular time of day. This was due to the fact that the tiny particles of dust were disrupting the path of the sunlight through the atmosphere. The dust also affected the moonlight. The moon looked hazy and took on a blue color.

Left *A rare German photograph of the eruption of Krakatoa in 1883.*

Inset *the wreckage of a ship carried 3 km (1.8 mi) inland by the giant wave.*

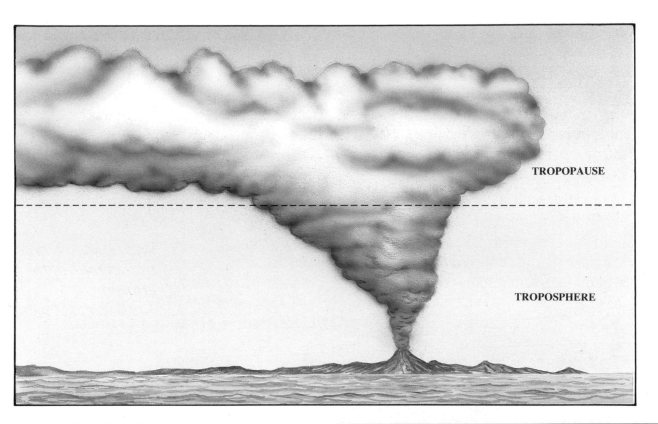

TROPOPAUSE

TROPOSPHERE

Above *The cloud thrown up by the eruption reached the layer of the atmosphere known as the tropopause, 18 km (11 mi) above the earth's surface. It was then blown around the world.*

Right *The extra dust in the atmosphere caused spectacular sunsets like this one photographed recently in India.*

The "impossible" event referred to in the well-known saying "once in a blue moon" became fact. This dust was thrown so high that three years passed before it settled completely. Never since has a volcanic eruption had such wide-ranging and long-term results.

KRAKATOA TODAY

Before the terrible explosion of 1883, Krakatoa covered an area of 29 square km (11 sq mi). Afterward, it measured only about 10 square km (4 sq mi) in extent. All life, whether plant or animal, was destroyed. Krakatoa lay as a lifeless rock.

However, plant seeds were carried to the island by the wind. They took root and soon a lush jungle covered the slopes of the remnants of Krakatoa. Animals such as birds and insects came to the island to take advantage of the rich plantlife. However, no people came to live on Krakatoa. They were afraid fresh eruptions might occur and destroy their homes once again.

In 1927, Krakatoa became volcanically active once again. However, there was no repetition of the events of 1883. Instead, slow and steady eruptions piled up lava and ash to form a new island. This small island is known locally as Anak Krakatau, which means "Son of Krakatoa."

Few people visit the islands of Krakatoa and Anak Krakatau. Scientists come to the islands occasionally to set up equipment and take readings. These will help in the understanding of volcanic activity.

Below *The volcanic island of Anak Krakatau as it is today.*

Some tourists visiting Java are tempted to travel to view the scene of the tragedy. The only method of reaching the islands is to hire a boat from a nearby port, such as Labauan on Java. The trip takes several hours, and few people make the effort. Those that do arrive find steep-sided islands rising sheer from the sparkling ocean. Steam and smoke still rise from time to time from the new volcanic cone, a constant reminder of the terrible devastation that once occurred there.

Above *The 1927 eruption that created Anak Krakatau.*

Right *The sun shines on villages and paddies in western Java. Many survivors of the eruption found new homes here.*

GLOSSARY

Atomic bomb An extremely destructive bomb. Its power is created by the splitting of an atom — a process known as nuclear fission.

Caldera A volcanic crater that has been enlarged by eruptions occurring after the one that created it.

Crater The depression, usually circular, that is caused by a volcanic eruption.

Dormant Asleep. The word is used to describe a volcano that has not erupted for some time.

Dutch colonial government The people in charge of Indonesia at the time of the eruption.

Earth's crust The outer layer of the earth, from 10 km (6 mi) to 40 km (25 mi) deep.

Export To sell or transport goods to a foreign place.

Fertile Very productive. Plants grow well on fertile soil.

Geological plate A section of the earth's crust. Volcanoes often occur where two or more geological plates meet.

Indonesia A group of islands between Southeast Asia and Australia. For many years the islands were ruled by the Dutch.

Last Judgement The occasion when, according to the Bible, God will decide who will go to heaven, who to hell.

Lava Extremely hot, molten rock that may pour out of volcanoes during an eruption.

Monsoon A period of the year in which there is much heavier rainfall than at other times. In Indonesia this occurs during the summer.

Outrigger A long piece of wood attached to the side of a canoe by long struts in order to make the canoe more stable.

Paddy A field of rice.

Refugee A person whose home has been destroyed by warfare or natural disaster and who is forced to move to somewhere safe.

Ritual dancing A type of dancing that is performed to a set pattern that may be determined by religious or other ceremonies.

Tsunami The Japanese name used to describe large ocean waves caused by earthquakes or volcanic eruptions. The word is now used by scientists throughout the world.

Volcano A fault in the earth's crust through which hot lava, ash and gases may erupt.

Xylophone A percussion instrument consisting of a set of wooden bars of different lengths. It is played by hitting the bars with special hammers.

BOOKS TO READ

Disastrous Volcanoes, by Melvin Berger. Franklin Watts, 1981
Geological Disasters: Earthquakes and Volcanoes by Thomas G. Aylesworth.
   Franklin Watts, 1979
Great Disasters by Andrew Langley. The Bookwright Press, 1986
Mountains and Earth Movements, by Iain Bain. The Bookwright Press, 1984
Volcanoes, by James Carson. The Bookwright Press, 1984
Volcanoes and Earthquakes by Martyn Bramwell. Franklin Watts, 1986

IMPORTANT DATES

c. 1,000,000 B.C. Krakatoa formed.
c. 3,000 B.C. First humans arrive on Krakatoa.
A.D. 1681-1883 Krakatoa dormant.
May 20, 1883 Krakatoa erupts, pouring out ash and smoke.
August 26, 1883 Violent explosion shakes Krakatoa.
August 27, 1883 Massive explosion. Most of Krakatoa sinks beneath the sea.
1927 Krakatoa comes alive again. Anak Krakatau formed.
1988 Anak Krakatau active: frequent eruptions and tremors.

INDEX

ACKNOWLEDGMENTS

The illustrations on pages 4-5, 6-7, 17, 18-19, 22-3, 25 and on the cover are by Tony Smith. The illustrations on pages 8, 12, 13, 15, 20, 21 and 27 are by Peter Bull.

The publishers would like to thank the following for providing the photographs in this book: Aerofilms 29 (t); Chapel Studios 27 (b); BBC Hulton 10 (t), 15 (t), 26; Bruce Coleman 28; Douglas Dickins 10 (b), 11 (b); ET Archive 14 (t), 16 (b); Mary Evans 24 (b); Geoscience Features 17 (t); Hutchison 9 (b), 11 (t); Tony Stone 9 (t), 13 (b), 14 (b), 16 (t), 29 (b); Wayland 21 (t).